EXCEL

The Ultimate Comprehensive Step-by-Step
Guide to the Basics of Excel Programming

Kevin Clark

TABLE OF CONTENTS

Introduction

VBA is a tool that helps you perform tasks in the easiest way possible. You can perform these tasks in less than a minute when you automate them using VBA. For instance, you can create custom reports, add new toolbars or perform different types of data analysis using VBA. If you want to gather more information on VBA programming, you have come to the right place. This book provides more information about VBA and also talks about the different ways you can use VBA to automate processes.

Over the course of the book, you will gather information on conditional and looping statements, arrays, strings and other necessary information. You will also learn how to redirect the flow of programs and also how you should handle any errors. There are a few examples that have been given across the book. You should practice these examples before you begin writing your code.

Thank you for purchasing the book. I hope you gather all the information you are looking for.

Chapter 1:

Introduction to VBA

Visual Basic for Applications or VBA is a programming language that is compatible with most Microsoft Office Products, including Excel. In other words, you can use VBA to develop programs in Excel. These programs will make Excel operate accurately and very fast.

What can you do with VBA?

Most people use Excel for a million different reasons. Here are a few examples:

1. Forecasting and Budgeting

2. Analyzing data

3. Developing diagrams and charts using data

4. Creating lists

5. Creating forms and invoices

This list is endless, but I am sure you get the idea. In other words, you can use Excel to perform a variety of tasks, and I am sure you are reading this book because you have a set of expectations. If you want to automate the functions of Excel, you should use VBA.

For instance, you may want to create or develop a program that will help you import some data or numbers and then format that data to print a report. Once you develop the code, you can execute the macro using a command or a button. This will ensure that Excel performs the task in a few seconds or minutes.

Common Uses of VBA

You must understand why you want to use VBA. You must ensure that you can take some time out of your busy schedule to sit down and write a VBA code. You must understand the different tasks you can use VBA for. You cannot use VBA to perform your chores, but you can use it to make some tasks easier for you. This section covers some tasks that you can perform with VBA.

Automating Documents

Most people do not like to prepare documents, and if these documents contain the same information, they will not want to work on each document. You can use the Excel Ad-in called Mail Merge to automate letters, but this is not an option to use when you want to write individual letters or documents. In such situations, you can use a VBA code to create a form that will include the common information. You can include check boxes that VBA will use to write the document for you.

Word processing is not the only task you can automate using VBA. You can also automate the spreadsheet and there are numerous programs you can create for the same. For example, you can extract information or data from the Internet into a spreadsheet by clicking a button. Therefore, you can limit the time you spend on simply copying the data from the web and pasting it according to the required format in your Excel worksheet.

Customizing Application Interfaces

There are times when the features of an application will bug you, and you can turn off those features. But, that is not an option if you want to use that feature in your work. Instead of disabling that feature, you can use VBA to create a new feature that has all the functions that you need. For instance, instead of using conditional formatting every time you need to make changes in a worksheet, you can write a VBA code to do that for you.

It is easy to change the interface of an application, so it works better for you. You can customize toolbars or menu systems, and can also move some elements around in the interface to make it look presentable. Additionally, you can use multiple interfaces and use a VBA code to shift between those interfaces.

One of the most common applications of VBA is to perform a variety of calculations. You can create different equations and graphs using the data you obtain. You may have to make changes to the data so you can perform some calculations on it. If you find that an equation is complicated, you can use VBA to simplify the process. You can also use iterative functions to perform a calculation.

There are times when the results of a calculation do not mean too much. This value is simply a number and nothing more than that until someone makes a decision to use that number. There are times when the decisions being taken are repetitive.

Adding new application features

Most vendors or developers never use the applications they build. Therefore, they never update the code for their applications. You can add new features to the application using VBA codes and work on developing an application. When you develop applications that complete some of your work in a few minutes, you will impress your boss and colleagues. This is an added advantage to using VBA.

Chapter 2:

Recording a Macro

Microsoft Office products like PowerPoint, Word, Outlook, FrontPage, Visio, Access, Project, Excel and some other third-party programs support VBA. If you have Microsoft Office on your device, you have VBA. VBA works similarly on all Microsoft products except for Access. The differences only relate to the specific objects of every application. For example, if you are using a spreadsheet object, you can only use it in Excel. VBA is currently based on VB 6.0, but there is a possibility that the future releases will migrate towards .net.

The focus of this book is how you can use VBA in Excel. VBA enhances the use of Excel by providing valuable features that you will not find with Excel formulas.

Macro Recorder

You can write macros in VBA in the same way that you would write a code in VB. The concepts of structures, variables, expressions, sub procedures, etc. are the same for both VB and VBA. The problem with VBA is that you will need to refer to every object you are writing a code for. For example, if you were writing a code for a specific cell in a worksheet, you will need to refer to that specific cell in your code. You are often unaware of what the names of these objects are and the attributes that you can control. The Macro Recorder solves this problem.

The macro recorder helps you develop a new macro in Excel quickly and easily. You must start the recorder and perform the necessary actions. The macro recorder will write the code for you. Alternatively, you can also run the VBA editor, which will allow you to insert a new module. This will give you a blank sheet on which you can write your macro. If you have already written the macro, you do not have to insert a new module. You will only need to add code to an existing module.

You will need to make some changes to the code written by the macro recorder. You should do this when you need to change the cell references from absolute to relative or when you need the user form to interact with the user. If you have read the earlier version of the book, you will be familiar with VBA in Excel and some of the syntaxes and structures. Additionally, you must understand the differences between relative and absolute addressing.

VBA is different from VB in the sense that it is not a standalone language. VBA can only run through another product. For example, every VBA application you write in Excel can only run within Excel, which means that you should always open Excel, load the macro and then compile the macro. The VBA applications are all stored in the spreadsheet that they were written in. You can also store VBA application in a way that will allow you to refer to them in other worksheets or workbooks.

When the application is loaded into Excel, you can invoke the application in many ways. Let us look at a few ways to run the macro:

Step One

You can assign a key to the macro when you record the macro. You can then invoke the macro by pressing Ctrl-"key." If the key is "a," your shortcut will be Ctrl+a. You must remember that the macro shortcut will override the default meaning of the Ctrl+a shortcut. You should also note that Ctrl/a and Ctrl/A are different.

Step Two

You can either include an object or a button on the spreadsheet to call the macro. Go to the Forms window using the path Menu->View->Toolbars->Forms and select the command button. Now, draw the button on the spreadsheet. Choose the macro that you want to link to the button when the dialog box or prompt opens. You can also include pictures and other objects and assign macros to them.

Step Three

Select the macro from the menu and run it. Go to the Macros section using the following path Menu->Tools->Macro->Macros and choose the macro you want to run.

Step Four

You can also use the VBA editor to run the macro. You can either click on the run button to run the macro or go through each line of the code while giving yourself time to debug the code. When you are debugging the code, you should move the VBA editor into a pane adjacent to the spreadsheet and execute the code to see what is happening.

If you choose to name a macro "Sub Auto_Open()," this macro will run when you load or open the spreadsheet. This will only happen if you have enabled macros.

Security and Macro Storage

For every Microsoft Office application, there are three security levels for macros. The macro security level is always set to high by default. To change the security of your macro, go to the security tab and make your selection. Go to Menu->Tools->Security Tab->Macro Security.

The three security levels for macros are:

- High: The macros that are signed by a trusted source will run in Excel. If there is any unsigned macro, it will automatically be disabled.

- Medium: This is the recommended setting since you can choose to enable or disable a macro.

- Low: This is not recommended since the macros are loaded into the workbook without notifying the user.

If you know you will be using macros, you should set the security of the macros to medium. When you load the spreadsheet, Excel will ask you if you want to enable or disable a macro. If you know that a specific sheet contains a macro and you know who wrote it, you can enable it.

Since there are some macros that are set to run when you open a spreadsheet, it is not possible for you to always have the chance to examine the macro before you enable it. It is important to remember that an Excel Macro virus is very rare because a macro is only available on the spreadsheet where it was written. Macros are always stored in the workbook by default and every time you load the workbook, the macros are loaded.

When you create a macro for the first time, you can decide where to store the macro. The best choices are:

1. This Workbook: The macro is stored in the worksheet where it is written. Anybody who has access to the worksheet can access the macro.

2. Personal Macro Workbook: All the macros on your PC are stored in this workbook. Only when you copy the macro and save it with the spreadsheet will others be able to view the macro.

You can use the VBA editor to see where the macros are stored. The Project Explorer Window, on the upper left of the screen, shows you where the files are placed and their hierarchy. You can use the Explorer to view, move, copy or delete a macro.

Chapter 3:

How to Use Data from Excel

You may not want to manually copy records from one Excel file to another. If you automate this procedure, you can ensure that the data is entered accurately, there is no duplication in the data and the figures will not be entered in an incorrect location. This will also save time.

You can write the code to perform this function in the Workbook_Open() event or function in ThisWorkBook object in VBA. When you write this code in the Workbook_Open() function, the compiler will ensure that the figures are updated correctly when the source Excel file is open.

To develop the code, open the destination excel file and press Alt+F8. You will find the ThisWorkBook module under the Microsoft Excel Objects in Project Explorer. Open the window and from the object dropdown list, choose "Workbook."

Option Explicit

Private Sub Workbook_Open()

```vba
    Call ReadDataFromCloseFile

End Sub


Sub ReadDataFromCloseFile()

    On Error GoTo ErrHandler

    Application.ScreenUpdating = False

        Dim src As Workbook

        ' OPEN THE SOURCE EXCEL WORKBOOK IN
"READ ONLY MODE".

    Set src = Workbooks.Open("C:\Q-SALES.xlsx",
True, True)

        ' GET THE TOTAL ROWS FROM THE SOURCE
WORKBOOK.

    Dim iTotalRows As Integer

    iTotalRows =
src.Worksheets("sheet1").Range("B1:B" &
Cells(Rows.Count, "B").End(xlUp).Row).Rows.Count

        ' COPY DATA FROM SOURCE (CLOSE
WORKGROUP) TO THE DESTINATION
WORKBOOK.

        Dim iCnt As Integer       ' COUNTER.

    For iCnt = 1 To iTotalRows
```

```
        Worksheets("Sheet1").Range("B" & iCnt).Formula
=

        src.Worksheets("Sheet1").Range("B" &
iCnt).Formula

    Next iCnt

        ' CLOSE THE SOURCE FILE.

    src.Close False            ' FALSE - DON'T SAVE THE
SOURCE FILE.

    Set src = Nothing

    ErrHandler:

    Application.EnableEvents = True

    Application.ScreenUpdating = True

End Sub
```

Property Application.ScreenUpdating

In the first line of the code, you will see that the Application.ScreenUpdating property is set to false. This is done to increase the speed of the macro that you have written.

Open the Source File and Read Data

We are then opening the source workbook to read or copy the data from it. Excel will only open the file in the read only state. This means that it will make no changes to the source file.

Set src = Workbooks.Open("C:\Q-SALES.xlsx", True, True)

Once you have obtained the data, the compiler will count the number of rows present in the source workbook. The loop will run and the data will be copied from the source and pasted into the destination workbook.

```
' COPY DATA FROM SOURCE (CLOSE
WORKGROUP) TO THE DESTINATION FILE.

For iCnt = 1 To iTotalRows

   Worksheets("Sheet1").Range("B" & iCnt).Formula =

      src.Worksheets("Sheet1").Range("B" &
iCnt).Formula

Next iCnt
```

You should then close the source file and finally set the property Application.ScreenUpdating to true.

Chapter 4:

How to Manipulate Data in Excel

A macro processes code written in the Visual Basic Editor to manage and manipulate huge volumes of data. The previous chapter provides information on how you can use a macro to format certain fields or cells in Excel to meet your criteria.

Let us look at the VBA script below:

```
Sub ConfigureLogic()

Dim qstEntries

Dim dqstEntries

Dim qstCnt, dqstCnt

qstEntries = Range("QualifiedEntry").Count

qst = qstEntries -
WorksheetFunction.CountIf(Range("QualifiedEntry"),
"")

ReDim QualifiedEntryText(qst)

'MsgBox (qst)
```

```
dqstEntries = Range("DisQualifiedEntry").Count

dqst = dqstEntries -
WorksheetFunction.CountIf(Range("DisQualifiedEntry
"), "")

ReDim DisqualifiedEntryText(dqst)

'MsgBox (dqst)

For qstCnt = 1 To qst

QualifiedEntryText(qstCnt) =
ThisWorkbook.Worksheets("Qualifiers").Range("J" &
8 + qstCnt).value

'MsgBox (QualifiedEntryText(qstCnt))

logging ("Configured Qualified Entry entry #" & qstCnt
& " as {" & QualifiedEntryText(qstCnt) & "}")

Next

For dqstCnt = 1 To dqst

DisqualifiedEntryText(dqstCnt) =
ThisWorkbook.Worksheets("Qualifiers").Range("M" &
8 + dqstCnt).value

'MsgBox (DisqualifiedEntryText(dqstCnt))

logging ("Configured DisQualified Entry entry #" &
qstCnt & " as {" & DisqualifiedEntryText(dqstCnt) &
"}")
```

Next

```
includeEntry =
ThisWorkbook.Worksheets("Qualifiers").Range("Includ
eSibling").value
```

'MsgBox (includeEntry)

logging ("Entrys included in search - " & includeEntry)

End Sub

How to Analyze and Manipulate Data in a Spreadsheet

If you want to use VBA to analyze data, you should check the macro settings in Excel. Ensure that the settings as per your requirements. You should also make sure that the macro settings are activated in Excel. Now, create a worksheet and call it 'Qualifiers.' We will be using this worksheet to check the data and ensure that the data qualifies all the selections that you require. You must then set up the qualifiers based on the code you have written. You cannot cut and paste these qualifiers, but will need to enter them manually.

```
ThisWorkbook.Worksheets("Qualifiers").Range("J" &
8 + qstCnt).value
```

How to Construct an Array and Locate the Range

In the above function, the range will start from Cell J9. The function notes 8, but the range is 9 since we have declared the qstCnt to be 1 using the following code:

For qstCnt = 1 To qst

It is because of this statement that the list will start at 9.

If you want to construct an array using the entries in the Qualifiers worksheet, you should add random words or numbers between cells J9 and J13, including those cells. When the rows are complete, you can find and manipulate the data in Excel.

```
Private Sub CountSheets()

Dim sheetcount

Dim WS As Worksheet

sheetcount = 0

logging ("*****Starting Scrub*********")

For Each WS In ThisWorkbook.Worksheets

sheetcount = sheetcount + 1

If WS.Name = "Selected" Then

'need to log the date and time into sheet named "Logging"
```

```
ActionCnt = ActionCnt + 1

logging ("Calling sheet: " & WS.Name)

scrubsheet (sheetcount)

Else

ActionCnt = ActionCnt + 1

logging ("Skipped over sheet: " & WS.Name)

End If

Next WS

'MsgBox ("ending")

ActionCnt = ActionCnt + 1

logging ("****Scrub DONE!")

Application.ScreenUpdating = True

End Sub
```

You can use the example below to write a macro to create a working tab counter.

```
Dim sheetcount

Dim WS As Worksheet

sheetcount = 0

logging ("*****Starting Scrub*********")
```

```
For Each WS In ThisWorkbook.Worksheets
```

```
sheetcount = sheetcount + 1
```

When you initialize the sheet count variable, you should first set it to zero before you restart the counter. You can also use the logging() subroutine to keep track of all the actions in the qualifiers tab to make the correct selections. The For loop in the above example will set up the counting variable in the Active Workbook. Once you initialize WS, it will make the worksheet that you are currently in the active worksheet. Since this module is unnamed, it will run in any workbook. If you have many workbooks open, this module may run in an incorrect workbook. If you want to avoid any errors, you should name the workbook that you want the module to run in.

When the loop runs, it will add another variable to the sheet count and keep a track of the tabs. We will then move to

```
If WS.Name = "Selected" Then
```

```
'need to log the date and time into sheet named "Logging"
```

```
ActionCnt = ActionCnt + 1
```

```
logging ("Calling sheet: " & WS.Name)
```

```
scrubsheet (sheetcount)
```

```
Else
```

```
ActionCnt = ActionCnt + 1
```

```
logging ("Skipped over sheet: " & WS.Name)
```

```
End If
```

In this section of the code, we are looking for the Selected tab. If the variable WS is the same as the Selected worksheet, you can fire the Scrub sheet subroutine. If the variable WS is not the same as the Selected worksheet, then the sheet will be skipped and the action will be counted. The code above is an example of how you can write a macro to count the number of tabs and locate a specific tab.

The next parts of this chapter talk about the different ways you can manipulate data in Excel.

Different Ways to Manipulate Data

Count The Number Of Sheets In A Workbook

```
Dim TAB
```

```
For Each TAB In ThisWorkbook.Worksheets
```

```
'some routine here
```

```
Next
```

Filter By Using Advanced Criteria

Range("A2:Z99").Sort key1:=Range("A5"), order1:=xlAscending, Header:=xlNo

Find The Last Column, Cell Or Row On A Worksheet

Dim cellcount

cellcount = Cells(ThisWorkbook.Worksheets("worksheet").Rows.Count, 1).End(xlUp).Row

Getting Values From Another Worksheet

dim newvalue

newvalue = ThisWorkbook.Worksheets("worksheet").Range("F1").value

Apply Auto-Fit To A Column

Columns("A:A").EntireColumn.AutoFit

Adding Named Ranges to Specific Sheets

ThisWorkbook.Worksheets("worksheet").Names.Add Name:="Status", RefersToR1C1:="=worksheet!C2"

Insert Rows Into A Worksheet

Dim Row, Column

Cells(Row, Column).EntireRow.Select

```vb
Selection.Insert
```

Copy An Entire Row For Pasting

```vb
ActiveSheet.Range("A1").EntireRow.Select

Selection.Copy
```

Delete an Entire Row

```vb
ActiveSheet.Range("A1").EntireRow.Select

Selection.Delete
```

Inserting A Column Into A Worksheet

```vb
Dim Row, Column

Cells(Row, Column).EntireColumn.Select

Selection.Insert
```

Insert Multiple Columns Into A Worksheet

```vb
Dim insertCnt

Dim Row, Column

For insertCnt = 1 To N

ThisWorkbook.Worksheets("worksheet").Select

Cells(Row, Column).EntireColumn.Select

Selection.Insert

Next
```

Select A Specific Sheet

ThisWorkbook.Worksheets("worksheet").Select

Compare Values In A Range

Dim firstrange

Dim Logictest

Logictest = "some word or value"

If (Range(firstrange).value = Logictest) then

'some routine here

End If

Chapter 5:

Working With Loops

One of the most powerful and basic programming tools available in VBA is a loop. This tool is used across many programming languages where the programmer wants to repeat a block of code until a condition holds true or until a specific point. If the condition is false, the loop will break and the section of code after the loop is executed. By using loops, you can write a few lines of code and achieve significant output.

The For Loop

For…Next Statement

The For…Next Loop will repeat a statement or a block of code for a specific number of iterations. You will need to use the following syntax for the loop:

For counter_variable = start_value To end_value

[block of code]

Next counter_variable

Let us look at a simple example of how to use this loop.

```
Sub forNext1()

Dim i As Integer

Dim iTotal As Integer

iTotal = 0

For i = 1 To 5

iTotal = i + iTotal

Next i

MsgBox iTotal

End Sub
```

The For Each ... Next Statement

If you want to repeat a block of code for every object or variable in a group, you should use the For Each...Next Loop. This statement will repeat the execution of a block of code or statements for every element in the collection. The loop will stop when every element in the collection is covered. The execution will immediately move to that section of code that is immediately after the Next statement. The syntax of the loop is as follows:

```
For Each object_variable In group_object_variable

[block of code]

Next object_variable
```

Example 1

In the example below, the loop will go through every worksheet in the workbook. VBA will execute the code which will protect the worksheets with a password. In this example, the variable is the Worksheet Object variable. The group or collection of worksheets is present in this workbook.

```
Sub forEach1()

Dim ws As Worksheet

For Each ws In ThisWorkbook.Worksheets

ws.Protect Password:="123"

Next ws

End Sub
```

Example 2

In the example below, the VBA will iterate through every cell in the range A1:A10. The code will set the background color of every cell to yellow. In this example, rCell is the Range Object variable, and the collection or group of cells is present in Range("A1:A10").

```
Sub forEach2()

Dim rCell As Range
```

```vba
For Each rCell In ActiveSheet.Range("A1:A10")

rCell.Interior.Color = RGB(255, 255, 0)

Next rCell

End Sub
```

Nesting Loops

If you want to include more than one condition in a loop, you can use nesting. You can create a nested loop by adding one loop to another. You can add an infinite number of loops if you are creating a nested loop. You can also nest one type of a loop inside another type of loop.

If you are using a For Loop, the inner loop must be completed first. It is only after the inner loop is fully complete that the statements below the Next statement of the inner loop are executed. Alternatively, you can nest one type of control structure in another.

In the example below, we will use an IF statement in a WITH statement that is within a For...Each Loop. VBA will go through every cell in the range A1:A10. If the value of the cell exceeds 5, VBA will color the cell as Yellow. Otherwise, it will color the cells red.

```vba
Sub nestingLoops()

Dim rCell As Range

For Each rCell In ActiveSheet.Range("A1:A10")
```

```
With rCell

If rCell > 5 Then

.Interior.Color = RGB(255, 255, 0)

Else

.Interior.Color = RGB(255, 0, 0)

End If

End With

Next rCell

End Sub
```

The Exit For Statement

You can use the Exit For statement to exit the For Loop without completing the full cycle. This means that you will be exiting the For Loop early. This statement will instruct VBA to stop the execution of the loop and move to the section or block of code at the end of the loop, or the code that follows the Next statement. If you are using Nested loops, VBA will stop the execution of the code in the inner level and move to the outer level. You should use this statement wen you want to terminate the loop once it has satisfied a condition or reached a specific value. You can also use this statement to break an endless loop after a certain point.

Let us look at the following example:

In the example below, if the value of Range("A1") is blank, the value of the variable iTotal will be 55. If Range("A1") has the value 5, VBA will terminate the loop when the counter reaches the value 5. At this point, the value of iTotal will be 15. You should note that the loop will run until the counter value reaches 5, after which it will exit the loop.

```
Sub exitFor1()

Dim i As Integer

Dim iTotal As Integer

iTotal = 0

For i = 1 To 10

iTotal = i + iTotal

If i = ActiveSheet.Range("A1") Then

Exit For

End If

Next i

MsgBox iTotal

End Sub
```

The Do While Loop

You can use the Do While Loop to repeat a block of code or statements indefinitely as long as the condition is met and the value is True. VBA will stop executing the block of code when the condition returns the value False. You can test the condition either at the start or at the end of the loop. The Do While...Loop statement is where the condition is tested at the start while the Do...Loop While statement is the condition that is tested at the end of the loop. When the condition at the start of the loop is not met, the former loop will not execute the block of code in the loop. The latter statement will function at least once since the condition is at the end of the loop.

Do While...Loop Statement

The syntax for the loop is:

Do While [Condition]

[block of code]

Loop

Do...Loop While Statement

The syntax for the loop is:

Do

[block of code]

Loop While [Condition]

The loops are explained below with the help of examples.

Example 1

In the example below, the condition is tested at the beginning of the loop. Since the condition is not met, the loop will not execute, and the value of iTotal will be zero.

```
Sub doWhile1()

Dim i As Integer

Dim iTotal As Integer

i = 5

iTotal = 0

Do While i > 5

iTotal = i + iTotal

i = i - 1

Loop

MsgBox iTotal

End Sub
```

Example 2

In the example below, the condition is only tested at the end of the function. Since the condition is true, the loop will execute once. It will terminate after that since the value of I will reduce to 4, and the variable iTotal will return the value 5.

```
Sub doWhile2()

Dim i As Integer

Dim iTotal As Integer

i = 5

iTotal = 0

Do

iTotal = i + iTotal

i = i - 1

Loop While i > 5

MsgBox iTotal

End Sub
```

Example 3

In this example, we will replace the blanks in a range of cells with underscores.

```vba
Sub doWhile3()

Dim rCell As Range

Dim strText As String

Dim n As Integer

'rCell is a Cell in the specified Range which contains the strText

'strText is the text in a Cell in which blank spaces are to be replaced with underscores

'n is the position of blank space(s) occurring in a strText

For Each rCell In ActiveSheet.Range("A1:A5")

strText = rCell

'the VBA InStr function returns the position of the first occurrence of a string within another string. Using this to determine the position of the first blank space in the strText.

n = InStr(strText, " ")

Do While n > 0

'blank space is replaced with the underscore character in the strText

strText = Left(strText, n - 1) & "_" & Right(strText, Len(strText) - n)
```

'Use this line of code instead of the preceding line, to remove all blank spaces in the strText

'strText= Left(strText, n - 1) & Right(strText, Len(strText) - n)

n = InStr(strText, " ")

Loop

rCell = strText

Next

End Sub

The Exit Do Statement

You can use the Exit Do Statement to exit the Do While Loop before you complete the cycle. The Exit Do statement will instruct VBA to stop executing the lines of code in the loop and move to the block of code that is immediately after the loop. If it is a nested loop, the statement will instruct VBA to execute the lines of code in the outer loop. You can use an infinite number of Exit Do statements in a loop, and this statement is useful when you want to terminate the loop once you obtain the desired value. This is similar to the Exit For statement.

Let us look at the following example. In the example below, the iTotal will be 55 is Range("A1") is blank. If it contains the number 5, VBA will terminate the loop when the value of the counter is 5. The value of iTotal will increase to 10.

```
Sub exitDo1()

Dim i As Integer

Dim iTotal As Integer

iTotal = 0

Do While i < 11

iTotal = i + iTotal

i = i + 1

If i = ActiveSheet.Range("A1") Then

Exit Do

End If

Loop

MsgBox iTotal

End Sub
```

The Do Until Loop

When you use the Do Until Loop, VBA will repeat the block of code indefinitely until the specified condition is true. You can use this statement to test the condition either at the start or at the end of the loop. The Do

Until…Loop statement will test the condition at the start of the loop while the Do…Loop Until statement will test the condition at the end of the loop. In the former statement, if the condition is false, VBA will not execute the block of code within the statement since the condition has to hold true from the start. In the latter statement, the block of code in the loop will execute at least once since the condition is at the end of the loop.

Do Until…Loop Statement

The syntax for the statement is below:

Do Until [Condition]

[block of code]

Loop

Let us look at the following statements using the following examples.

Example 1

In this example, VBA will color every empty cell yellow until it encounters a non-empty cell. If there is a non-empty cell at the start, the code will not execute since the condition is mentioned at the beginning of the loop.

```
Sub doUntil1()

Dim rowNo As Integer

rowNo = 1

Do Until Not IsEmpty(Cells(rowNo, 1))
```

```vba
Cells(rowNo, 1).Interior.Color = RGB(255, 255, 0)

rowNo = rowNo + 1

Loop

End Sub
```

Example 2

In this example, VBA will color every empty cell yellow until it encounters a non-empty cell. If there is a non-empty cell at the start, the code will execute at least once since the condition is mentioned at the end of the loop.

```vba
Sub doUntil2()

Dim rowNo As Integer

rowNo = 1

Do

Cells(rowNo, 1).Interior.Color = RGB(255, 255, 0)

rowNo = rowNo + 1

Loop Until Not IsEmpty(Cells(rowNo, 1))

End Sub
```

The Exit Do Statement

You can use the Exit Do statement to exit the Do Until Loop without completing a full cycle. This is similar to the Do While Loop that we looked at earlier.

Chapter 6:

Working with
Conditional Statements

There are two conditional statements that you can use in VBA:

1. If…Then…Else

2. Select…Case

In both these conditional statements, VBA will need to evaluate one or more conditions after which the block of code between the parentheses is executed. These statements are executed depending on what the result of the evaluation is.

If…Then…Else Statements

This conditional statement will execute a block of statements or code when the condition is met.

Multiple-line Statements

If condition Then

statements

ElseIf elseif_condition_1 Then

elseif_statements_1

ElseIf elseif_condition_n Then

elseif_statements_n

Else

else_statements

End If

Let us break the statements down to understand what each part of the block of code written above means.

If Statement

If you want to write a multiple-line syntax, like the example above, the first line of the code should only contain the 'If' statement. We will cover the single-line syntax in the following section.

Condition

This is an expression that could either be a string or numeric. The compiler will evaluate this condition and return either true or false. It is necessary to define a condition.

Statements

These statements make up the block of code that the compiler will execute if the condition is true. If you do not specify a statement, then the compiler will not execute any code even if the condition is true.

ElseIf

This is a clause that can be used if you want to include multiple conditions. If you have an ElseIf in the code, you need to specify the elseif condition. You can include an infinite number of ElseIf and elseif conditions in your code.

elseif_condition

This is an expression that the compiler will need to evaluate. The result of the expression should either be true or false.

Elseif_statements

These statements or blocks of code are evaluated if the compiler returns the result true for the elseif condition. If you do not specify a statement, then the compiler will not execute any code even if the condition is true.

The Else -> condition and elseif_conditions are always tested in the order they are written in. If any condition is true, the block of code that comes immediately after the condition will be executed. If no conditions in the elseif_conditions returns the value the true, the block of code after the Else clause will be executed. You can choose to include the Else in the If...Then...Else statement.

else_statements

These statements are the blocks of code written immediately after the Else statement.

End If

This statement terminates the If…Then…Else block of statements and you must mention these keywords at the end of the block.

Nesting

You can nest the If…Then…Else statements in a loop using the Select…Case or VBA Loops (covered in the previous chapter), without a limit. If you are using Excel 2003, you can only use 7 levels of nesting, but if you use Excel 2007, you can use 64. The latest versions of Excel allow a larger level of nesting.

Let us look at the following example:

Example 1

Sub ElseIfStructure()

'Returns Good if the marks are equal to 60.

Dim sngMarks As Single

sngMarks = 60

If sngMarks >= 80 Then

MsgBox "Excellent"

ElseIf sngMarks >= 60 And sngMarks < 80 Then

MsgBox "Good"

ElseIf sngMarks >= 40 And sngMarks < 60 Then

MsgBox "Average"

Else

MsgBox "Poor"

End If

End Sub

Example 2

In this example, we will use Multiple If...Then Statements. This is an alternative to the ElseIf structure, but is not as efficient as the ElseIf Structure. In the Multiple If...Then Statements, the compiler will need to run through every If...Then block of code even after it returns the result true for one of the conditions. If you use the ElseIf structure, the subsequent conditions are not checked if one condition is true. This makes the ElseIf structure faster. If you can perform the function using the ElseIf structure, you should avoid using the Multiple If...Then Structure.

Sub multipleIfThenStmnts()

"Returns Good if the marks are equal to 60.

Dim sngMarks As Single

```
sngMarks = 60

If sngMarks >= 80 Then

MsgBox "Excellent"

End If

If sngMarks >= 60 And sngMarks < 80 Then

MsgBox "Good"

End If

If sngMarks >= 40 And sngMarks < 60 Then

MsgBox "Average"

End If

If sngMarks < 40 Then

MsgBox "Poor"

End If

End Sub
```

Example 3

In this example, we will nest the If...Then...Else statements within a For...Next Loop.

```
Sub IfThenNesting()
```

'The user will need to enter 5 numbers. The compiler will add the even numbers and subtract the odd numbers.

```
Dim i As Integer, n As Integer, iEvenSum As Integer, iOddSum As Integer

For n = 1 To 5

i = InputBox("enter number")

If i Mod 2 = 0 Then

iEvenSum = iEvenSum + i

Else

iOddSum = iOddSum + i

End If

Next n

MsgBox "sum of even numbers is " & iEvenSum

MsgBox "sum of odd numbers is " & iOddSum

End Sub
```

Example 4

You can use the following options to test multiple variables using the If…Then statements.

Option 1: ElseIf Structure

```
Sub IfThen1()

'this procedure returns the message "Pass in maths and
Fail in science"

Dim sngMaths As Single, sngScience As Single

sngMaths = 50

sngScience = 30

If sngMaths >= 40 And sngScience >= 40 Then

MsgBox "Pass in both maths and science"

ElseIf sngMaths >= 40 And sngScience < 40 Then

MsgBox "Pass in maths and Fail in science"

ElseIf sngMaths < 40 And sngScience >= 40 Then

MsgBox "Fail in maths and Pass in science"

Else

MsgBox "Fail in both maths and science"

End If

End Sub
```

Option 2: If…Then…Else Nesting

```
Sub IfThen2()
```

'this procedure returns the message "Pass in maths and
Fail in science"

```
Dim sngMaths As Single, sngScience As Single

sngMaths = 50

sngScience = 30

If sngMaths >= 40 Then

If sngScience >= 40 Then

MsgBox "Pass in both maths and science"

Else

MsgBox "Pass in maths and Fail in science"

End If

Else

If sngScience >= 40 Then

MsgBox "Fail in maths and Pass in science"

Else

MsgBox "Fail in both maths and science"

End If

End If

End Sub
```

Option 3: Multiple If…Then Statements

As mentioned earlier, this may not be the best way to operate.

```
Sub IfThen3()

'this procedure returns the message "Pass in maths and
Fail in science"

Dim sngMaths As Single, sngScience As Single

sngMaths = 50

sngScience = 30

If sngMaths >= 40 And sngScience >= 40 Then

MsgBox "Pass in both maths and science"

End If

If sngMaths >= 40 And sngScience < 40 Then

MsgBox "Pass in maths and Fail in science"

End If

If sngMaths < 40 And sngScience >= 40 Then

MsgBox "Fail in maths and Pass in science"

End If

If sngMaths < 40 And sngScience < 40 Then

MsgBox "Fail in both maths and science"

End If

 End Sub
```

Example 5

In this example, we will use the If Not, If IsNumeric and IsEmpty functions in the Worksheet_Change event.

Private Sub Worksheet_Change(ByVal Target As Range)

'Using If IsEmpty, If Not and If IsNumeric (in If…Then statements) in the Worksheet_Change event.

'auto run a VBA code, when content of a worksheet cell changes, with the Worksheet_Change event.

On Error GoTo ErrHandler

Application.EnableEvents = False

'if target cell is empty post change, nothing will happen

If IsEmpty(Target) Then

Application.EnableEvents = True

Exit Sub

End If

'using If Not statement with the Intersect Method to determine if Target cell(s) is within specified range of "B1:B20"

If Not Intersect(Target, Range("B1:B20")) Is Nothing Then

'if target cell is changed to a numeric value

```
If IsNumeric(Target) Then

'changes the target cell color to yellow

Target.Interior.Color = RGB(255, 255, 0)

End If

End If

Application.EnableEvents = True

ErrHandler:

    Application.EnableEvents = True

    Exit Sub

End Sub
```

Using the Not Operator

When you use the Not operator on any Boolean expression, the compiler will reverse the true value with the false value and vice versa. The Not operator will always reverse the logic in any conditional statement. In the example above, If Not Intersect(Target, Range("B1:B20")) Is Nothing Then means If Intersect(Target, Range("B1:B20")) Is Not Nothing Then or If Intersect(Target, Range("B1:B20")) Is Something Then. In simple words, this means that the condition should not be true if the range falls or intersects between the range ("B1:B20").

Single Line If…Then…Else Statements

If you are writing a short or simple code, you should use the single-line syntax. If you wish to distinguish between the singly-line and multiple-line syntax, you should look at the block of code that succeeds the Then keyword. If there is nothing succeeding the Then keyword, the block of code is multiple-line. Otherwise, it is a single-line code.

The syntax for Single-line statements is as follows:

If condition Then statements Else else_statements

These blocks of statements can also be nested in a single-line syntax within each other. You can insert the clause Else If in the code, which is similar to the ElseIf clause. You do not need to use the End If keywords in the single-syntax block of code since the program will automatically terminate.

Let us look at some examples where we will use the single-line syntax for the If…Then…Else statements.

If sngMarks > 80 Then MsgBox "Excellent Marks"

If sngMarks > 80 Then MsgBox "Excellent Marks" Else MsgBox "Not Excellent"

'add MsgBox title "Grading":

If sngMarks > 80 Then MsgBox "Excellent Marks", , "Grading"

'using logical operator And in the condition:

```
If sngMarks > 80 And sngAvg > 80 Then MsgBox
"Both Marks & Average are Excellent" Else MsgBox
"Not Excellent"
```

'nesting another If...Then statement:

```
If sngMarks > 80 Then If sngAvg > 80 Then MsgBox
"Both Marks & Average are Excellent"
```

Example 1

```
Sub IfThenSingleLine1()

Dim sngMarks As Single

sngMarks = 85
```

'Execute multiple statements / codes after Then keyword. Code will return 3 messages: "Excellent Marks - 85 on 90"; "Keep it up!" and "94.44% marks".

```
If sngMarks = 85 Then MsgBox "Excellent Marks - 85
on 90": MsgBox "Keep it up!": MsgBox Format(85 / 90
* 100, "0.00") & "% marks"

End Sub
```

Example 2

```
Sub IfThenSingleLine1()

Dim sngMarks As Single

sngMarks = 85
```

'Execute multiple statements / codes after Then keyword. Code will return 3 messages: "Excellent Marks - 85 on 90"; "Keep it up!" and "94.44% marks".

If sngMarks = 85 Then MsgBox "Excellent Marks - 85 on 90": MsgBox "Keep it up!": MsgBox Format(85 / 90 * 100, "0.00") & "% marks"

End Sub

Example 3

Sub IfThenSingleLine2()

Dim sngMarks As Single, sngAvg As Single

sngMarks = 85

sngAvg = 75

'nesting If...Then statements. Code will return the message: "Marks are Excellent, but Average is not"

If sngMarks > 80 Then If sngAvg > 80 Then MsgBox "Both Marks & Average are Excellent" Else MsgBox "Marks are Excellent, but Average is not" Else MsgBox "Marks are not Excellent"

End Sub

Example 4

Sub IfThenSingleLine3()

Dim sngMarks As Single

sngMarks = 65

'using the keywords Else If (in single-line syntax), similar to ElseIf (in multiple-line syntax). Procedure will return the message: "Marks are Good".

If sngMarks > 80 Then MsgBox "Marks are Excellent" Else If sngMarks >= 60 Then MsgBox "Marks are Good" Else If sngMarks >= 40 Then MsgBox "Marks are Average" Else MsgBox "Marks are Poor"

End Sub

Select…Case Statement

The Select…Case statement will execute statements or a block of code depending on whether some conditions have been met. It will evaluate an expression and executes one of the many blocks of code depending on the result of the expression. This statement is similar to the If…The…Else statement.

Syntax

Select Case expression

Case expression_value_1

statements_1

Case expression_value_n

statements_n

Case Else

else_statements

End Select

Expression

This can be a range, field or a variable. The expression can be expressed by using a VBA function -> as "rng.HasFormula" or "IsNumeric(rng)" where the 'rng' is the range variable. The expression can return a String value, Boolean Value, Numeric Value or any other data type. It is important that you specify the expression. It is the value of the expression that the compiler will test and compare with each case in the Select...Case statement. When the values match, the compiler will execute the block of code under the matching Case.

Expression_value

The data type of the expression_value should be the same as the expression or a similar data type. The compiler will compare the value of the expression against the expression_value in each case. If it finds a match, the block of code under the case or the statements will be executed. You must specify at least one expression_value, and the compiler will test the expression against these values in the order they are mentioned in. The expression_values are similar to a list of conditions where the condition must be met for the relevant block of code to be executed.

Statements

The compiler will execute the block of code or statements under a specific case if the value of the expression and the expression_value are the same.

Case Else -> expression_value

When the compiler matches the value of the expression to the expression_value, it will execute the block of code under that case. It will not check the value of the expression against the remaining expression_value. If the compiler does not find a match against any expression_value, it will move to the Case Else clause. The statements under this clause are executed. You do not have to use this clause when you write your code.

Else_statements

As mentioned earlier, the else_statements are included in the Case Else section of the code. If the compiler cannot match the value of the expression to any expression_value, it will execute these statements.

End Select

These keywords terminate the Select…Case block of statements. You must mention these keywords at the end of the Select…Case statements.

Let us look at an example of the Select…Case statements.

Sub selectCase1()

'making strAge equivalent to "young" will return the
message "Less than 40 years"

Dim strAge As String

strAge = "young"

Select Case strAge

Case "senior citizen"

MsgBox "Over 60 years"

Case "middle age"

MsgBox "Between 40 to 59 years"

Case "young"

MsgBox "Less than 40 years"

Case Else

MsgBox "Invalid"

End Select

End Sub

Using the To Keyword

You can use the To keyword to specify the upper and
lower range of all matching values in the
expression_value section of the Select…Case
statements. The value on the left side of the To keyword
should either be less than or equal to the value on the

right side of the To keyword. You can also specify the range for a specified set of characters.

Let us look at an example.

```
Sub selectCaseTo()

'entering marks as 69 will return the message "Average"; entering marks as 101 will return the message "Out of Range"

Dim iMarks As Integer

iMarks = InputBox("Enter marks")

Select Case iMarks

Case 70 To 100

MsgBox "Good"

Case 40 To 69

MsgBox "Average"

Case 0 To 39

MsgBox "Failed"

Case Else

MsgBox "Out of Range"

End Select

End Sub
```

Using the Is Keyword

You can use the Is keyword if you want to include a comparison operator like <>, ==, <=, >=, < or >. If you do not include the Is keyword, the compiler will automatically include it. Let us look at the example below.

Sub selectCaseIs()

'if sngTemp equals 39.5, returned message is "Moderately Hot"

Dim sngTemp As Single

sngTemp = 39.5

Select Case sngTemp

Case Is >= 40

MsgBox "Extremely Hot"

Case Is >= 25

MsgBox "Moderately Hot"

Case Is >= 0

MsgBox "Cool Weather"

Case Is < 0

MsgBox "Extremely Cold"

End Select

End Sub

Using a comma

You can include multiple ranges or expressions in the Case clause. These ranges and expressions can be separated with a comma. The comma acts like the OR operator. You can also specify multiple expressions and ranges for character strings. Let us look at the example below.

Example 1

Sub selectCaseMultiple_1()

'if alpha equates to "Hello", the returned message is "Odd Number or Hello"

Dim alpha As Variant

alpha = "Hello"

Select Case alpha

Case a, e, i, o, u

MsgBox "Vowels"

Case 2, 4, 6, 8

MsgBox "Even Number"

Case 1, 3, 5, 7, 9, "Hello"

MsgBox "Odd Number or Hello"

Case Else

```
MsgBox "Out of Range"

End Select

End Sub
```

Example 2

In this example, we are comparing the strings "apples" to "grapes." The compiler will determine the value between "apples" and "grapes" and will use the default comparison method binary.

```
Sub
SelectCaseMultiple_OptionCompare_NotSpecified()

'Option Compare is NOT specified and therefore text
comparison will be case-sensitive

'bananas will return the message "Text between apples
and grapes, or specifically mangoes, or the numbers 98
or 99"; oranges will return the message "Out of Range";
Apples will return the message "Out of Range".

Dim var As Variant, strResult As String

var = InputBox("Enter")

Select Case var

Case 1 To 10, 11 To 20: strResult = "Number is
between 1 and 20"
```

Case "apples" To "grapes", "mangoes", 98, 99: strResult = "Text between apples and grapes, or specifically mangoes, or the numbers 98 or 99"

Case Else: strResult = "Out of Range"

End Select

MsgBox strResult

End Sub

Nesting

You can nest the Select…Case block of code or statements within VBA loops, If…Then…Else statements and within a Select…Case block. There is no limit on the number of cases you can include in the code. If you are nesting a Select…Case within another Select…Case, it should be a complete block by itself and also terminate with its End Select.

Example 1

```
Sub selectCaseNested1()
```

'check if a range is empty; and if not empty, whether has a numeric value and if numeric then if also has a formula; and if not numeric then what is the text length.

```
Dim rng As Range, iLength As Integer

Set rng = ActiveSheet.Range("A1")
```

```vba
Select Case IsEmpty(rng)

Case True

MsgBox rng.Address & " is empty"

Case Else

Select Case IsNumeric(rng)

Case True

MsgBox rng.Address & " has a numeric value"

Select Case rng.HasFormula

Case True

MsgBox rng.Address & " also has a formula"

End Select

Case Else

iLength = Len(rng)

MsgBox rng.Address & " has a Text length of " & iLength

End Select

End Select

End Sub
```

Example 2

Function StringManipulation(str As String) As String

'This code customizes a string text as follows:

'1. removes numericals from a text string;

'2. removes leading, trailing & inbetween spaces (leaves single space between words);

'3. adds space (if not present) after each exclamation, comma, full stop and question mark;

'4. capitalizes the very first letter of the string and the first letter of a word after each exclamation, full stop and question mark;

 Dim iTxtLen As Integer, iStrLen As Integer, n As Integer, i As Integer, ansiCode As Integer

'----------------------------

'REMOVE NUMERICALS

'chr(48) to chr(57) represent numericals 0 to 9 in ANSI/ASCII character codes

For i = 48 To 57

'remove all numericals from the text string using vba Replace function:

str = Replace(str, Chr(i), "")

Next i

'---------------------------

'REMOVE LEADING, TRAILING & INBETWEEN SPACES (LEAVE SINGLE SPACE BETWEEN WORDS)

'use the worksheet TRIM function. Note: the TRIM function removes space character with ANSI code 32, does not remove the nonbreaking space character with ANSI code 160

str = Application.Trim(str)

'---------------------------

'ADD SPACE (IF NOT PRESENT) AFTER EACH EXCLAMATION, COMMA, DOT AND QUESTION MARK:

'set variable value to string length:

iTxtLen = Len(str)

For n = iTxtLen To 1 Step -1

'Chr(32) returns space; Chr(33) returns exclamation; Chr(44) returns comma; Chr(46) returns full stop; Chr(63) returns question mark;

If Mid(str, n, 1) = Chr(33) Or Mid(str, n, 1) = Chr(44) Or Mid(str, n, 1) = Chr(46) Or Mid(str, n, 1) = Chr(63) Then

'check if space is not present:

If Mid(str, n + 1, 1) <> Chr(32) Then

'using Mid & Right functions to add space - note that current string length is used:

str = Mid(str, 1, n) & Chr(32) & Right(str, iTxtLen - n)

'update string length - increments by 1 after adding a space (character):

iTxtLen = iTxtLen + 1

End If

End If

Next n

'----------------------------

'DELETE SPACE (IF PRESENT) BEFORE EACH EXCLAMATION, COMMA, DOT & QUESTION MARK:

'reset variable value to string length:

iTxtLen = Len(str)

For n = iTxtLen To 1 Step -1

'Chr(32) returns space; Chr(33) returns exclamation; Chr(44) returns comma; Chr(46) returns full stop; Chr(63) returns question mark;

```vba
If Mid(str, n, 1) = Chr(33) Or Mid(str, n, 1) = Chr(44)
Or Mid(str, n, 1) = Chr(46) Or Mid(str, n, 1) = Chr(63)
Then
```

'check if space is present:

```vba
If Mid(str, n - 1, 1) = Chr(32) Then
```

'using the worksheet Replace function to delete a space:

```vba
str = Application.Replace(str, n - 1, 1, "")
```

'omit rechecking the same character again - position of n shifts (decreases by 1) due to deleting a space character:

```vba
n = n - 1
```

```vba
End If
```

```vba
End If
```

```vba
Next n
```

'----------------------------

'CAPITALIZE LETTERS:

'capitalize the very first letter of the string and the first letter of a word after each exclamation, full stop and question mark, while all other letters are lower case

```vba
iStrLen = Len(str)
```

```vba
For i = 1 To iStrLen
```

'determine the ANSI code of each character in the string

ansiCode = Asc(Mid(str, i, 1))

Select Case ansiCode

'97 to 122 are the ANSI codes equating to small cap letters "a" to "z"

Case 97 To 122

If i > 2 Then

'capitalizes a letter whose position is 2 characters after (1 character after, will be the space character added earlier) an exclamation, full stop and question mark:

If Mid(str, i - 2, 1) = Chr(33) Or Mid(str, i - 2, 1) = Chr(46) Or Mid(str, i - 2, 1) = Chr(63) Then

Mid(str, i, 1) = UCase(Mid(str, i, 1))

End If

'capitalize first letter of the string:

ElseIf i = 1 Then

Mid(str, i, 1) = UCase(Mid(str, i, 1))

End If

'if capital letter, skip to next character (ie. next i):

Case Else

```vba
GoTo skip

End Select

skip:

Next i

'---------------------------

'manipulated string:

StringManipulation = str

End Function

Sub Str_Man()

'specify text string to manipulate & get manipulated string

Dim strText As String

'specify the text string, which is required to be manipulated

strText = ActiveSheet.Range("A1").Value

'the manipulated text string is entered in range A5 of the active sheet, on running the procedure:

ActiveSheet.Range("A5").Value                    = StringManipulation(strText)

End Sub
```

Go To Statement

You can use the Go To statement to move to a different section of the code or jump a line in the procedure. There are two parts to the Go To statement:

- The GoTo keywords that are followed by an identifier, also known as the Label.

- The Label, which is followed by a colon and the line of code or a few statements.

If the value of the expression satisfies the condition, the compiler will move to a separate line of code that is indicated in the GoTo statement. You can avoid this statement and use the If...Then...Else statement. The Go To function makes the code unreadable and confusing.

Select...Case Statements Versus the If...Then...Else Statements

The Select...Case and If...Then...Else statements are both conditional statements. In each of these statements either one or more conditions are tested and the compiler will execute the block of code depending on what the result of the evaluation is.

The difference between the two statements is that in the Select...Case statement only one condition is evaluated at a time. The variable that is to be evaluated is initialized or declared in the Select Case expression.

The multiple case statements will specify the different values that the variable can take. In the If...Then...Else statement, multiple conditions can be evaluated and the code for different conditions can be executed at the same time.

The Select...Case statement will only test a single variable for several values while the If...Then...Else statement will test multiple variables for different values. In this sense, the If...Then... Else statement is more flexible since you can test multiple variables for different conditi0ns.

If you are testing a large number of conditions, you should avoid using the If...Then...Else statements since they may appear confusing. These statements can also make it difficult for you to read the code.

Chapter 7:

Working With Strings

S trings are an integral part of VBA, and every programmer will need to work with strings when he or she begins to automate functions using VBA. There are different types of manipulations that one can do on strings including

1. Extracting some parts of a string

2. Comparing different strings

3. Converting a number into a string

4. Formatting dates to include weekdays

5. Finding the characters in a string

6. Removing the blanks in a string

7. Parsing the string into an array

There are many functions in VBA that you can use to perform these tasks. This chapter will act as a guide on how you can work with strings in VBA. There are some simple examples in the book that you can practice.

Points to Remember

There are two points that you need to keep in mind when you work with strings.

Original String Does Not Change

You must remember that the original string function does not change when you perform some operations on strings. VBA returns a new string with all the changes you have made to it. If you want to make a change to the original string, you should assign the result of the function to the original string. We will cover this concept later in this chapter.

Comparing Two Strings

There are some string functions like Instr() and StrComp() that allow you to include the **Compare** parameter. This parameter works in the following way:

- **vbTextCompare**: The upper and lower case letters in the string are considered the same.

- **vbBinaryCompare**: The upper and lower case letters in the string are treated differently.

Let us look at the following example to see how you can use the Compare parameter in the StrComp() function.

Sub Comp1()

' Prints 0 if the strings do not match

Debug.Print   StrComp("MARoon",   "Maroon",
vbTextCompare)

' Prints 1 if the strings do not match

Debug.Print   StrComp("Maroon",   "MAROON",
vbBinaryCompare)

End Sub

Instead of using the same parameter every time, you can use the Option Compare. This parameter is defined at the top of any module, and a function that includes the parameter Compare will use this setting as its default. You can use the Option Compare in the following ways:

Option Compare Text

This option makes uses the vbTextCompare as the default compare argument.

Option Compare Text

Sub Comp2()

' Strings match - uses vbCompareText as Compare argument

Debug.Print StrComp("ABC", "abc")

Debug.Print StrComp("DEF", "def")

End Sub

Option Compare Binary

This option uses the vbBinaryCompare as the default compare argument.

Option Compare Binary

Sub Comp2()

    ' Strings do not match - uses vbCompareBinary as Compare argument

    Debug.Print StrComp("ABC", "abc")

    Debug.Print StrComp("DEF", "def")

End Sub

If you do not use the Option Compare statement, VBA uses Option Compare Binary as the default. Please keep these points in mind when we look at the individual string functions.

Appending Strings

You can use the & operator to append strings in VBA. Let us look at some examples of how you can use this operator to append strings.

Sub Append()

    Debug.Print "ABC" & "DEF"

    Debug.Print "Jane" & " " & "Smith"

Debug.Print "Long " & 22

Debug.Print "Double " & 14.99

Debug.Print "Date " & #12/12/2015#

End Sub

In the example above, there are different types of data that we have converted to string using the quotes. You will see that the plus operator can also be used to append strings in some programs. The difference between using the & operator and + operator is that the latter will only work with string data types. If you use it with any other data type, you will get an error message.

' You will get the following error: "Type Mismatch"

Debug.Print "Long " + 22

If you want to use a complex function to append strings, you should use the Format function which is described later in this chapter.

Extracting Parts of a String

In this section, we will look at some functions that you can use to extract information or data from strings.

You can use the Right, Left and Mid functions to extract the necessary parts in a string. These functions are simple to use. The Right function reads the sentence from the right, the Left function reads the sentence from the left and the Mid function will read the sentence from the point that you specify.

```vba
Sub UseLeftRightMid()

    Dim sCustomer As String

    sCustomer = "John Thomas Smith"

    Debug.Print Left(sCustomer, 4)  ' This will print John

    Debug.Print Right(sCustomer, 5) ' This will print Smith

    Debug.Print Left(sCustomer, 11)  ' This will print John Thomas

    Debug.Print Right(sCustomer, 12)  ' This will print Thomas Smith

    Debug.Print Mid(sCustomer, 1, 4) ' This will print John

    Debug.Print Mid(sCustomer, 6, 6) ' This will print Thomas

    Debug.Print Mid(sCustomer, 13, 5) ' This will print Smith

End Sub
```

As mentioned earlier, the string functions in VBA do not change the original string but return a new string as the result. In the following example, you will see that the string "FullName" remains unchanged even after the use of the Left function.

```
Sub UsingLeftExample()

    Dim Fullname As String

    Fullname = "John Smith"

    Debug.Print "Firstname is: "; Left(Fullname, 4)

    ' The original string remains unchanged

    Debug.Print "Fullname is: "; Fullname

End Sub
```

If you wish to make a change to the original string, you will need to assign the return value of the function to the original string.

```
Sub ChangingString()

    Dim name As String

    name = "John Smith"

    ' The return value of the function is assigned to the original string

    name = Left(name, 4)

    Debug.Print "Name is: "; name

End Sub
```

Searching in a String

InStr and InStrRev are two functions that you can use in VBA to search for substrings within a string. If the compiler can find the substring in the string, the position of the string is returned. This position is the index from where the string starts. If the substring is not found, the compiler will return zero. If the original string and substring are null, the value null is returned.

InStr

Description of Parameters

The function is written as follows:

InStr() Start[Optional], String1, String2, Compare[Optional]

1. **Start**: This number specified where the compiler should start looking for the substring within the actual string. The default option is one.

2. **String1**: This is the original string.

3. **String2**: This is the substring that you want the compiler to search for.

4. **Compare**: This is the method we looked at in the first part of this chapter.

The Use and Examples

This function will return the first position in the string where the substring is found. Let us look at the following example:

Sub FindSubString()

  Dim name As String

  name = "John Smith"

  ' This will return the number 3 which indicates the position of the first h

  Debug.Print InStr(name, "h")

  ' This will return the number 10 which indicates the position of the first h starting from position 4

  Debug.Print InStr(4, name, "h")

  ' This will return 8

  Debug.Print InStr(name, "it")

  ' This will return 6

  Debug.Print InStr(name, "Smith")

  ' This will return zero since the string "SSS" was not found

  Debug.Print InStr(name, "SSS")

End Sub

InStrRev

Description of Parameters

The function is written as follows:

InStrRev() StringCheck, StringMatch, Start[Optional], Compare[Optional]

1. **StringCheck**: This is the string that you need to search for.

2. **StringMatch**: This is the string the compiler should look for.

3. **Start**: This number specified where the compiler should start looking for the substring within the actual string. The default option is one.

4. **Compare**: This is the method we looked at in the first part of this chapter.

The Use and Examples

This function is the same as the InStr function except that is starts the search from the end of the original string. You must note that the position that the compiler returns is the position from the start of the sentence. Therefore, if the substring is available only once in the sentence, the InStr() and InStrRev() functions return the same value.

Let us look at some examples of the InStrRev function.

Sub UsingInstrRev()

```vba
Dim name As String

name = "John Smith"

' Both functions will return 1 which is the position of
the only J

Debug.Print InStr(name, "J")

Debug.Print InStrRev(name, "J")

' This will return 10 which indicates the second h

Debug.Print InStrRev(name, "h")

' This will return the number 3 and it indicates the
first h as searches from position 9

Debug.Print InStrRev(name, "h", 9)

' This will return 1

Debug.Print InStrRev(name, "John")

End Sub
```

You should use the InStr and InStrRev functions when you want to perform basic searches in strings. If you want to extract some text from a string, the process is slightly complicated.

Removing Blanks

In VBA, you can use the trim functions to remove blanks or spaces either at the start or end of a string.

The Use and Examples

- **Trim**: Removes the spaces from both the right and left of a string.

- **LTrim**: Removes the spaces only from the left of the string.

- **RTrim**: Removes the spaces from the right of the string.

```
Sub TrimStr()

    Dim name As String

    name = "  John Smith  "

    ' Will print "John Smith  "

    Debug.Print LTrim(name)

    ' Will print "  John Smith"

    Debug.Print RTrim(name)

    ' Will print "John Smith"

    Debug.Print Trim(name)

End Sub
```

Length of a String

You can use Len to return the length of the string since it is a simple function. This function will return the number of characters in the string. If you use different numeric data types like long, the function will return the number of bytes in the string.

```
Sub GetLen()

    Dim name As String

    name = "John Smith"

    ' This will print 10

    Debug.Print Len("John Smith")

    ' This will print 3

    Debug.Print Len("ABC")

    ' This will print 4 since the numeric data type Long is
4 bytes in size

    Dim total As Long

    Debug.Print Len(total)

End Sub
```

Reversing a String

The StrReverse function is another easy function to use. This will return the original string with the characters reversed.

```
Sub RevStr()
```

```
Dim s As String

s = "Jane Smith"

' This will print htimS enaJ

Debug.Print StrReverse(s)
```
End Sub

Comparing Strings

You can use the function StrComp to compare two strings.

Description of Parameters

The function is written as follows:

StrComp() String1, String2, Compare[Optional]

- **String1**: The first string that needs to be compared.

- **String2**: The second string that needs to be compared.

- **Compare**: This is the method we looked at in the first part of this chapter.

The Use and Examples

Let us look at some examples of how to use the StrComp function:

Sub UsingStrComp()

  ' This will return 0

  Debug.Print StrComp("ABC", "ABC", vbTextCompare)

  ' This will return 1

  Debug.Print StrComp("ABCD", "ABC", vbTextCompare)

  ' This will return -1

  Debug.Print StrComp("ABC", "ABCD", vbTextCompare)

  ' This will return Null

  Debug.Print StrComp(Null, "ABCD", vbTextCompare)

End Sub

Comparing Strings Using Operators

VBA allows you to use the equal to sign to compare two strings. The differences between the StrComp and equal to sign are:

1. The equal to sign will return either true or false.

2. You cannot combine a Compare parameter with the equal sign since it will only use the Option Compare setting.

Let us look at a few examples where we use the equal to sign to compare two strings.

```
Option Compare Text

Sub CompareUsingEquals()

    ' This will return true

    Debug.Print "ABC" = "ABC"

    ' This will return True since the compare text
parameter is at the start of the program

    Debug.Print "ABC" = "abc"

    ' This will return false

    Debug.Print "ABCD" = "ABC"

    ' This will return false

    Debug.Print "ABC" = "ABCD"

    ' This will return null

    Debug.Print Null = "ABCD"

End Sub
```

To see if two strings are not equal, you must use the "<>" operator. This operator performs a function that is opposite to the equal to sign.

Option Compare Text

```vba
Sub CompareWithNotEqual()

    ' This will return false

    Debug.Print "ABC" <> "ABC"

    ' This will return false since the Compare Text
    parameter is at the start of the program

    Debug.Print "ABC" <> "abc"

    ' This will return true

    Debug.Print "ABCD" <> "ABC"

    ' This will return true

    Debug.Print "ABC" <> "ABCD"

    ' This will return null

    Debug.Print Null <> "ABCD"

End Sub
```

Comparing Strings Using Pattern Matching

Pattern matching is a VBA technique that helps you
determine if a string has a specific pattern of characters.
For instance, there are times when you need to check if
a customer number has 3 numeric values and 3
alphabetic characters or if a specific string has the
letters ABC followed by a set of numbers or characters.
If the compiler deems that the string matches the

pattern, it will return the value "True", otherwise, it will return the value "False."

Pattern matching is similar to the Format function. This means that you can use pattern matching in multiple ways. In this section, we will look at some examples that will help you understand how the pattern matching technique works. This will cover the common uses of pattern matching. Let us take the following string: [abc][!def]]?#X*

Let us look at how this string will work:

- [abc]: This will represent a character – a, b or c.

- [!def]: This will represent a character that is not d, e or f.

- ?: This will represent any character.

- #: This will represent any digit.

- X: This represents the character X.

- *: This means that the string is followed by more characters or zero.

Therefore, this is a valid string.

Now, let us consider the following string: apY6X.

1. a: This character is one of a, b and c.

2. p: This is not a character that is d, e or f.

3. Y: This is any character.

4. 6: This is a digit.

5. X: This is the letter X.

You can now say that the pattern for both strings is the same.

Let us look at a code that will show you a variety of results when you use the same pattern:

Sub Patterns()

   ' This will print true

   Debug.Print 1; "apY6X" Like "[abc][!def]?#X*"

   ' This will print true since any combination is valid after X

   Debug.Print 2; "apY6Xsf34FAD" Like "[abc][!def]?#X*"

   ' This will print false since the character is not a, b or c

   Debug.Print 3; "dpY6X" Like "[abc][!def]?#X*"

   ' This will print false since the character is one of d, e and f

   Debug.Print 4; "aeY6X" Like "[abc][!def]?#X*"

   ' This will print false since the character at 4 should be a digit.

Debug.Print 5; "apYAX" Like "[abc][!def]?#X*"

' This will print false since the character at position 5 should be X.

Debug.Print 1; "apY6Z" Like "[abc][!def]?#X*"

End Sub

Replacing Part of a String

You should use the replace function when you want to replace a substring in a string using another substring. This function will replace all the instances where the substrings are found.

Description of Parameters

The function is written as follows:

Replace() Expression, Find, Replace, Start[Optional], Count[Optional], Compare[Optional]

- Expression: This is the original string.

- Find: This is the substring that you want to replace in the Expression string.

- Replace: This is the substring you want to replace the Find substring with.

- Start: This is the start position of the string. The position is taken as 1 by default.

- Count: This is the number of substitutions you want to make. The default is one, which means that all the Find substrings are replaced with the Replace substring.

- Compare: This is the method we looked at in the first part of this chapter.

The Use and Examples

In the following code, we will look at some examples of how to use the Replace function.

Sub ReplaceExamples()

    ' To replace all the question marks in the string with semi colons.

    Debug.Print Replace("A?B?C?D?E", "?", ";")

    ' To replace Smith with Jones

    Debug.Print Replace("Peter Smith,Ann Smith", "Smith", "Jones")

    ' To replace AX with AB

    Debug.Print Replace("ACD AXC BAX", "AX", "AB")

End Sub

The output will be as follows:

A;B;C;D;E

Peter Jones,Sophia Jones

ACD ABC BAB

In the next block of code, we will use the Count optional parameter to determine the number of substitutions you want to make. For instance, if you set up Count equal to one, it means that you want the compiler to only replace the first occurrence of the Find string.

Sub ReplaceCount()

    ' To replace only the first question mark

    Debug.Print Replace("A?B?C?D?E", "?", ";", Count:=1)

    ' To replace the first two question marks

    Debug.Print Replace("A?B?C?D?E", "?", ";", Count:=2)

End Sub

The output will be as follows:

A;B?C?D?E

A;B;C?D?E

You can return a part of the string if you use the Start optional parameter. The compiler will return the part of the string from the position that you specify in the Start parameter. When you use this operator, it will ignore all the words or the part of the string before the start position.

```
Sub ReplacePartial()

    ' This will use the original string from the position 4

    Debug.Print Replace("A?B?C?D?E", "?", ";", Start:=4)

    ' This will use the original string from the position 8

    Debug.Print Replace("AA?B?C?D?E", "?", ";", Start:=8)

    ' There are no items that will be replaced, but it will return the last two values

    Debug.Print Replace("ABCD", "X", "Y", Start:=3)

End Sub
```

The output will be as follows:

;C;D;E

;E

CD

There may be times when you want to replace only the lower or upper case letters in a string. At such times, you can use the Compare parameter. This is a parameter that can be used in many string functions. To understand this better, you should refer to the section above.

```
Sub ReplaceCase()

    ' This will only replace the capitalized A's

    Debug.Print Replace("AaAa", "A", "X",
Compare:=vbBinaryCompare)

    ' This will replace all the A's

    Debug.Print Replace("AaAa", "A", "X",
Compare:=vbTextCompare)

End Sub
```

The output is as follows:

XaXa

XXXX

Multiple Replaces

You can nest the calls if you want to replace more than one value in a string. Let us look at the following example where we will replace the X and Y with A and B respectively.

```
Sub ReplaceMulti()

    Dim newString As String

    ' Replace the A with X
```

```vba
newString = Replace("ABCD ABDN", "A", "X")

' Replace the B with Y in the new string

newString = Replace(newString, "B", "Y")

Debug.Print newString
End Sub
```

In the example below, we will make a few changes to the code above to perform this task. The return value of the first function is used as the argument or the original string for the second replacement.

```vba
Sub ReplaceMultiNested()

    Dim newString As String

    ' To replace A with X and B with Y

    newString = Replace(Replace("ABCD ABDN", "A", "X"), "B", "Y")

    Debug.Print newString
End Sub
```

The result of these replacements will be XYCD XYDN.

Chapter 8:

Error Handling and Debugging

Error handling is a common programming practice where the programmer should anticipate and code for error conditions, which may arise when he or she runs the program. You will come across three errors – user entry data errors where the user enters a negative number instead of a positive number, run time errors which occur when VBA cannot execute a program statement and compiler errors where the programmer has not declared a variable. We will only worry about the run time errors in this chapter since the other two errors are easy for a programmer to solve. Typical errors include those where VBA is attempting to access a worksheet or workbook that is non-existent or attempting to divide a number by zero. The code in this article will use try to divide a number by zero since we want to raise an error.

You should include as many checks as you can when you write the code to ensure that you do not come across any run time errors when you execute the code. This includes ensuring that the worksheets and workbooks being referred to in the code are all present and the names are defined. When you constantly check the application when you write the code, you can ensure that the macro is stable. This is better than to detect an error when your application is running.

If a run time error occurs and you do not have a code written to handle the errors, VBA will display the run time error dialog box. When the application is in the development stage, you can welcome these errors. If the application is at the final stage or in the production environment, you cannot expect to face these errors. The goal of an error handling code is to ensure that you identify the errors at run time and then correct them immediately. The goal should be to prevent the occurrence of any unhandled errors.

In this chapter, we will refer to Property procedure, Function and Sub as procedure and the words exit statement will mean Exit Property, Exit Function and Exit Sub. The words end statement will mean End Property, End Function, End Sub and End.

The On Error Statement

The heart of every error handling process in VBA is the On Error statement. When a run time error occurs, this statement will tell VBA what it must do to counter the error. The On Error statement takes the following forms:

- On Error Goto 0

- On Error Resume Next

- On Error Goto <label>:

On Error Goto o is the default in VBA. This statement indicates that VBA should always display the standard run time error dialog box if it encounters a run time error when it executes the code. This will give you a chance to enter the debug mode and check the code. Alternatively, you can terminate the code. The On Error Goto o is the same as not including an error handling statement in your code. The error will prompt VBA to display the standard window.

The On Error Resume Next is the most misused and commonly used form. This statement will instruct VBA to ignore the line of code that has the error and move to the next line of code. You must remember that this statement does not fix the code in any way. It will only tell VBA to act as if there was no error in the code. This error can have a negative effect on the code. It is important that you test your code for any errors and then take appropriate actions to solve those errors. You can do this by executing the appropriate code when the value of Err.Number is not zero. For instance,

On Error Resume Next

N = 1 / 0   ' cause an error

If Err.Number <> 0 Then

   N = 1

End If

In the above code, we are assigning the value of 1/0 to a variable N. This is an incorrect approach, therefore VBA will raise the Division By Zero Error (Error 11). The code will continue to execute since we have used the On Error Resume Next statement. The statement will assign a value to the variable N after it tests the value of Err.Number.

The third form is the On Error Goto <lable>. This statement will tell VBA that it needs to execute the line of code after a specific line label if an error occurs. When the error occurs, VBA will ignore every line of code between the error line and the specified line label, including any loop statements.

```
On Error Goto ErrHandler:

N = 1 / 0    ' cause an error

'

' more code

'

Exit Sub

ErrHandler:

' error handling code

Resume Next

End Sub
```

Enabled And Active Error Handlers

When the On Error statement is executed, VBA will enable an error handler. It is important to remember that VBA will only enable on error handler at any given point, and it will behave according to that error handler. VBA will execute the code in this error handler when any error occurs. The execution is transferred to a different location using the On Error Goto <label>: statement. The code in the error handler should either resume execution in the main program or fix the error in the program. You an also use the error handler to terminate the execution of the program. You cannot use it like the second form of the On Error statement to skip a few lines. For example, the code below will not function correctly:

```
On Error GoTo Err1:

Debug.Print 1 / 0

' more code

Err1:

On Error GoTo Err2:

Debug.Print 1 / 0

' more code

Err2:
```

The execution of code transfers to Err1 when the first error occurs. Since the error handler is active when the next error occurs, the On Error statement will not trap the error.

The Resume Statement

The Resume statement will instruct VBA to resume the execution of the code at a specific point the code. You should use the Resume statement only in the error handling blocks of code. If you use it in another part of the program, it will cause an error. You should not use the Goto statement to direct the code execution out of the error handling section of code. If you do this, you will encounter some strange problems with error handlers.

There are three syntactic forms that the Resume statement takes:

- Resume

- Resume Next

- Resume <label>

When Resume is used alone, it will instruct VBA to resume the execution of the program at the line of code that has the error. If you use this, you must ensure that the error handling code or block can fix the problem. Otherwise, the code will enter a loop that is endless since it will be jumping between the error handling block and the line that caused the error. In the example below, we will try to activate a worksheet that does not exist. VBA will give you an error (Subscript Out Of Range) and will immediately jump to the error handling code. This code will then create a sheet and solve the problems. The execution will then resume at the line of code that caused the error.

```
On Error GoTo ErrHandler:

Worksheets("NewSheet").Activate

Exit Sub

ErrHandler:

If Err.Number = 9 Then

    ' sheet does not exist, so create it

    Worksheets.Add.Name = "NewSheet"

    ' go back to the line of code that caused the
problem

    Resume

End If
```

The second form of the Resume is Resume Next. This statement will instruct VBA to execute the line of code that immediately follows the line that caused the error. The following code sets a value to the variable N and it causes an error. The error handling code will assign the variable N a value 1, and will continue to execute the remainder of the program.

```vba
On Error GoTo ErrHandler:

N = 1 / 0

Debug.Print N

Exit Sub

ErrHandler:

N = 1

' go back to the line following the error

Resume Next
```

The third form is the Resume <label> form. This is similar to the On Error Goto <label> statement. The statement will instruct VBA to execute the code from the line label. This means that it will skip the part of the code where there is an error. For instance,

```vba
On Error GoTo ErrHandler:

N = 1 / 0

'

' code that is skipped if an error occurs

'

Label1:
```

```
'
```

' more code to execute

```
'
```

Exit Sub

ErrHandler:

' go back to the line at Label1:

Resume Label1:

Every form of the Resume statement will either clear or reset the error object.

Error Handling With Multiple Procedures

You do not need to include an error code in every procedure. If an error occurs while running a program, VBA will use the last On Error statement and act accordingly. If the code that is causing the error is in the same procedure as the On Error statements, the error is handled in the ways mentioned above. If the procedure does not have an error handling code, VBA will need to go back to the procedure and proceed backward until it reaches the line with the incorrect code. For example, a procedure A calls B and B calls C, and only procedure A has an error handling code. If an error occurs in C, VBA will go back to the error handling code in procedure A. It will skip all the code in procedure B.

A Note Of Caution

You may want to use the On Error Resume Next statement when you are dealing with errors. This is a bad coding practice since you cannot run the code without solving the errors. You have to remember that this statement does not skip errors but ignores them.

Chapter 9:

How to Redirect the Flow

There are times when you will run into a situation where the program that you have written does not flow well. You may need to disrupt the code or will need to move the interpreter to another section of the code. It is a good idea to use the GoTo statement when you want to redirect the flow of the program. When you use this statement carefully, you will be able to overcome some programming problems. The GoTo statement will often cause more problems when compared to the other programming statement since most people misuse the statement. A novice programmer will find it easier to use this statement to overcome some issues. You should always use the GoTo statement with a lot of care. Therefore, you should work on designing the code so you can work on fixing the errors when you write the program.

Using the GoTo statement correctly

You can redirect the flow of your program using the GoTo statement. You will have come across this statement in different programs that you may have used in the past. That being said, it is important that you understand why you are using this statement, and also spend some time to identify other ways to redirect the flow of the program. You can redirect the flow by using a loop. You should only use the GoTo statement when you have run out of all options.

Loops

It is important to remember that you should never use the GoTo statement in a loop. You should always use the end statement to end the loop. The statements that you write within a loop will give another person an idea about the purpose of the loop. Additionally, when you use the end keyword in your loop, you can reduce the possibilities of creating an endless loop.

Exits

You should avoid using the GoTo statement when you want to exit a program. You can, however, use the End statement for the same task.

Program flow problems

You should always look at the pseudo-code to identify any problems that you may come across in the actual program. You must ensure that you design the program based on the pseudo-code that you have written at the start. You will also need to make changes to the design while working on developing the program. Ensure that you design the right pseudo-code, especially if you are working with VBA for the first time.

Chapter 10:

Mistakes to Avoid

I f you are reading this chapter, you will be familiar with Excel VBA. It is easy for anybody to make mistakes when they write a code in VBA. These mistakes will cost you greatly. This chapter lists the common mistakes that most VBA amateurs make.

Not Using Arrays

An interesting mistake that most VBA programmers make is that they try to process all the functions in a large nested loop. They filter the data down through the different rows and columns in the worksheet during the process of calculation. This method can work, but it can lead to performance troubles. If you have to perform the same function repeatedly, the efficiency of the macro will decrease. When you loop through the same column and you extract the values every single time, you are not only affecting the macro, but also affecting the processor. An efficient way to handle a list of numbers is to use an array.

If you have not used an array before, let me introduce it to you now. An array is a set of elements that have the same data type. Each element in the array is given an index. You must use this index to refer to the element in the array. An array can be defined by using the following statement: Dim MyArray (12) as Integer. This will create an array with 12 indices and variables that you will need to fill. Let us look at how a loop with an array will look like:

```
Sub Test1()

    Dim x As Integer

    intNumRows = Range("A2",
Range("A2").End(xldown)).Rows.Count

    Range("A2").Select

    For x = 1 To intNumRows

      arrMyArray(x-1) = Range("A" & str(x)).value)

      ActiveCell.Offset(1, 0).Select

    Next

  End Sub
```

In this example, the code is processing through every cell in the range before it performs the calculation function.

Using .Select or .Activate

You do not have to always use the .Select or .Activate functions when you write code in VBA. You may want to use these functions since the Macro Recorder generates them. These functions are unnecessary for the following reasons:

- These functions may lead to the repainting of the screen. If you use the following function Sheets("Sheet1").Activate, Excel will redraw the screen so you can see Sheet1. This will lead to a slow macro.

- These functions will confuse users since you will be manipulating the workbook when the user is working on it. There are some users who will worry that they are being hacked.

You should use these functions only when you want to bring the user to a specific cell or worksheet. Otherwise, you should delete the line of code since it will be doing more harm than good.

Using Variant Type

Another mistake that most programmers make is to use one Type when they are actually using another. If you look at the following code, you will think that a, b and c are of the Long type. Well, that is incorrect since the variables a and b are of the Variant type. This means that they can be any data type, and can change from one type to another.

It is dangerous to have a variant type since it will become difficult for you to identify the bugs in your code. You should always avoid Variant types in VBA. There are some functions that will need the use of a Variant type, but you should avoid them if you can.

Not Using Application.ScreenUpdating = False

When you make a change to a cell or a group of cells in your code, Excel will need to repaint the screen to show the user the changes. This will make your macros slow. When you write a macro the next time, you should use the following lines of code:

```
Public Sub MakeCodeFaster()

    Application.ScreenUpdating = False


    ' Block of code

    ' This setting should always be reset back

    Application.ScreenUpdating = True

End Sub
```

Referencing the Worksheet Name with a String

People will refer to a worksheet using a String. Look at the following example:

```
Public Sub SheetReferenceExample()

    Dim ws As Worksheet

    Set ws = Sheets("Sheet1")

    Debug.Print ws.Name

End Sub
```

This does seem harmless does it not? In most cases, it is harmless. Imagine that you give another person this workbook, and that person decides to rename the sheet to "Report." When he tries to run the macro, the macro will look for "Sheet1," which no longer exists. Therefore, this macro will not work. You should choose to reference the sheet by using an object instead of using the "Sheets" collection. To be more resilient, let us use the following block of code:

```
Public Sub SheetReferenceExample()

    Dim ws As Worksheet

    Set ws = Sheet1 ' used to be Sheets("Sheet1")

    Debug.Print ws.Name

End Sub
```

If you want to rename Sheet1 to something more meaningful, you can go to the VBA Project properties window and make a change to the name of the module. Once you rename the module, you will also need to update the VBA code.

Not Qualifying the Range References

This is a common mistake that most people make when they write their code, and it is a real pain to debug this error. This error comes up when you do not qualify the range reference in the VBA code. You may wonder what I mean when I say range reference.

When you say Range("A1"), which sheet do you think the code is referring to? It is referring to the Activesheet. This means that the compiler will look at cell A1 in the worksheet that the user is referring to. This is harmless on most occasions, but there are times when you may add more features to your code. These features make it hard for the compiler to execute the code. When the user or even you run the code, and you click on another worksheet, the code will behave differently. Let us look at the following example:

```
Public Sub FullyQualifyReferences()

    Dim fillRange As Range

    Set fillRange = Range("A1:B5")

    Dim cell As Range
```

```
For Each cell In fillRange

    Range(cell.Address) = cell.Address

    Application.Wait (Now + TimeValue("0:00:01"))

    DoEvents

  Next cell

End Sub
```

Run the code in VBA and see what happens. If you do not specify the worksheet when you use the Range() function, Excel will assume that you are looking at the active sheet. To avoid this, you should make a slight change to your code. All you need to do is change Range(cell.Address) = cell.Address to Data.Range(cell.Address) = cell.Address.

In the second statement, data refers to the sheet object. There are other ways to do this, but I wanted to use a simple example, which did not need the addition of too much code.

Writing a Big Function

If you go back to some of the old functions you may have written, you will notice that they are very long. You will need to continue to scroll until you reach the end of the function.

You should remember that the function you write should fit your screen. You should be able to view the code without having to scroll. You must ensure that you keep the methods short by creating sub procedures or helper functions.

Using Nested For or If Statements

You may have read earlier that you can include many levels of nesting when you write your code. Do you think that is a good idea? You will need to add comments and indent the code to ensure that another user can read your code. If you are unsure of what I mean by nesting, let us look at the following example:

```
Public Sub WayTooMuchNesting()

    Dim updateRange As Range

    Set updateRange = Sheet2.Range("B2:B50")

    Dim cell As Range

    For Each cell In updateRange

        If (cell.Value > 1) Then

            If (cell.Value < 100) Then

                If (cell.Offset(0, 1).Value = "2x Cost") Then

                    cell.Value = cell.Value * 2

                Else

                    ' do nothing
```

```
        End If

      End If

    End If

  Next cell

End Sub
```

This is certainly not a clean code. If you use more than three levels of nesting, you have gone too far. To reduce the number of nesting levels, you should invert the condition in your If statement. In the example above, the code will make a change if a bunch of statements pass. You can invert this to ensure that the compiler will only execute the statements for the opposite case. That way you can skip the many levels of nesting.

Let us look at the updated version of the above example.

```
Public Sub ReducedNesting()

  Dim updateRange As Range

  Set updateRange = Sheet2.Range("B2:B50")

  Dim cell As Range

  For Each cell In updateRange

    If (cell.Value <= 1) Then GoTo NextCell

    If (cell.Value >= 100) Then GoTo NextCell
```

```
    If (cell.Offset(0, 1).Value <> "2x Cost") Then
    GoTo NextCell

    cell.Value = cell.Value * 2

NextCell:

    Next cell

End Sub
```

You can also combine the If statements in the code above if you wish.

Conclusion

Thank you for purchasing the book.

If you want to master VBA, there are some concepts that you should know well. You should also have some tricks and tips up your sleeve to help you overcome any problems you may have with VBA. This book will help you master some of the concepts, and also leave you with some tips that you can use to troubleshoot and handle any errors and exceptions.

I hope the information in the book will help you improve your VBA programming skills.